TX
740.5
.S74
2016

Stepanova, Iryna, auth
photographer.
Tomato creatures : make your
own /

S0-BER-479

DATE DUE

WITHDRAWN

DEMCO 38-296

FASKEN LEARNING RESOURCE CENTER

9000087361

87361

Tomato Creatures

Make Your Own

Iryna Stepanova

Sergiy Kabachenko

FIREFLY BOOKS

Contents

Introduction

Food art. It's an amusing and engaging hobby – and not only for adults! Children will greatly enjoy "playing with their food" as they arrange fruits and vegetables of every color into various shapes and figures. And, if your child is too young to work with a knife, they will certainly enjoy putting the pieces together!

Tomatoes are an excellent source of vitamins, minerals and carbohydrates, whether cooked or raw. They come in many sizes, shapes and colors, and are known as a mood booster. These recipes let you combine fun and nutrition in one go.

To make the figures and shapes in this book, you don't need to have any special knowledge and culinary skill. The step-by-step illustrations will guide you through each transformation and make you a master of tomato food art.

Helpful tips:

- Choose the freshest and ripest tomatoes, the crispiest lettuce leaves and the brightest greens.
- Tomatoes should be properly washed, rinsed and dried with a clean towel before use.
- To keep lettuce leaves crisp, lay in a bowl and cover with cold water for several minutes. Rinse and dry with a clean towel.
- To keep tinned vegetables like sweet peas, beans and corn looking fresh, as well as green and black olives, you can toss them with a little olive oil. This will help them retain moisture and prevent them from wrinkling and growing dull.

Whimsical tomato food art can turn an everyday meal into a festive occasion, and make an indelible impression on your family and guests. Enjoy!

Peony

INGREDIENTS

1 tomato

green lettuce leaves

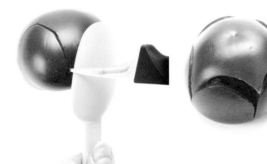

2 Carefully remove the top with your knife, trying not to touch the pulp in the middle of the tomato.

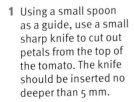

1 Using a small spoon as a guide, use a small sharp knife to cut out petals from the top of the tomato. The knife should be inserted no deeper than 5 mm.

3 Cut each petal in two by separating a thin layer of skin from the pulp. Turn out the external petals and lay the peony on the lettuce leaves.

Aster

INGREDIENTS

1 tomato
1 green chive stalk
corn kernels
watercress leaves

1 Starting at the top center of the tomato, cut very thin, downward slices almost to the base, inserting the knife no more than 5 mm, and creating approximately 20 petals.

2 Using the knife, separate each petal slightly from the internal pulp so that each is slightly extended.

3 Separate the skin on each petal from the pulp until they are all lying flat, then place some corn kernels in the center of the flower. Add the chive stalk as a stem, and decorate with watercress leaves.

Rose

INGREDIENTS

1 tomato

watercress leaves

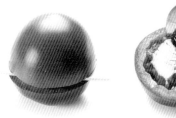

1 Cut off the bottom quarter from the base of the tomato.

2 Remove pulp with a spoon. This will be the cup for the petals.

3 Cut out a scalloped line of petals around the edge of the cup.

4 Slice the top part of the tomato very thinly, using a small, sharp knife.

5 Spread out the slices as shown in the image. These are the petals.

6 Carefully roll the strip of petals into a tight, spiral form.

7 Hold the spiral tightly together as you roll.

8 Place the petals in the cup and arrange as needed.

9 Decorate with watercress leaves.

Tulip

INGREDIENTS
1 tomato
2 snow peas
1 green chive stalk

1 Place the tomato on its base.

2 Make five equilateral incisions at the top center of the tomato.

3 Cut petals from the incisions to within 5 mm of the base.

4 Make the tops of the petals rounded.

5 Pierce a hole in the base of the tomato using a wooden skewer.

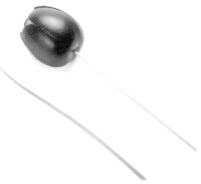 

6 Choose a chive stalk. This is the stem.

7 Insert the stem into the hole.

8 Put the pea pods against the stem to simulate leaves.

9 If desired, repeat steps 1 – 8 to make a bouquet of tulips.

Anthurium

INGREDIENTS

1 red tomato
1 small yellow tomato
green chive stalks
parsley leaves

1 Cut the red tomato in half.

2 Put each half with the cut side down.

3 Cut a section out of the center of each tomato half by making two symmetrical diagonal cuts.

4 Displace the cut section slightly.

5 Make a parallel cut toward the middle of the tomato slightly apart from the cut section.

6 Make the same cut to the middle of the tomato from the opposite side so that you can again cut out a section.

7 Displace it at the same distance as the first cut section.

8 Cut out one more section in the same manner.

9 Displace the last cut section. This is an anthurium.

10 Insert a chive stalk between the sections. This is the stem.

11 Cut a small segment out of a yellow tomato. This is the pistil.

12 Lay it in the middle of the flower. Decorate with parsley leaves.

Water Lily

INGREDIENTS

3 red tomatoes of different size (small, medium, large)

1 small yellow tomato (cherry or grape)

3 purple onion rings

lettuce leaves

1 Choose three tomatoes of different size.

2 In the large tomato, make six vertical cuts from the top center to within 5 mm of the base. These are the petals.

3 Unfold the petals carefully and cut out the pulp and seeds.

4 This is the lower layer of water lily petals.

5 Repeat steps 2-3 with the two smaller tomatoes. These are the middle and center petals.

6 Place the medium tomato on top of the large one.

7 If needed, use onion rings for stability.

8 Place the small tomato on top of the medium one.

9 Insert a small onion ring.

10 Set the yellow tomato in the flower. Make a lettuce bed.

Flower

INGREDIENTS

1 red tomato

1 onion ring

1 small yellow tomato

ramp (wild garlic) leaves

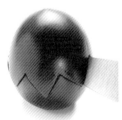

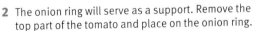

1 Using a small, sharp knife, make toothed incisions to the center of the tomato.

2 The onion ring will serve as a support. Remove the top part of the tomato and place on the onion ring.

3 Remove pulp. Place the yellow tomato in the middle. Decorate with ramp leaves.

Bellflowers

INGREDIENTS

4 small oval
   tomatoes

1 green chive stalk

corn kernels

ramp (wild garlic)
   leaves

1 Using a small, sharp knife, make toothed incisions to the center of the tomato.

2 Separate the tomato halves and remove the pulp. These are the bellflowers.

3 Insert a corn kernel into the center of the bellflower. Use the chive stalk as a stem. Decorate with ramp leaves as shown.

Butterfly

INGREDIENTS

2 red tomatoes

4 small yellow tomatoes

1 pitted green olive

1 whole black olive

green stalks of chive

lettuce leaves

1 Cut each red tomato into half. Place each half with the cut side down.

2 Cut a section out of the center of each tomato half by making two symmetrical diagonal cuts. Displace the cut section slightly.

3 Make a parallel cut lower and apart from the cut section. Repeat on the other side.

4 Displace it at the same distance as the first section.

5 Cut out one more section. Displace the last cut section. This is a butterfly wing.

6 Make three additional wings from the remaining tomato halves.

7 Use one yellow tomato for the head and the other three for the body.

8 Cut two rings from the green olive. Lay them on the head. These are eyes.

9 Cut the ends off the black olive. These are pupils. Lay them on top of the eyes.

10 Cut a chive stalk in half to use as antennae and place against the head.

11 Make legs by cutting an additional chive stalk into smaller pieces.

Owl

INGREDIENTS

2 red round tomatoes
1 red oval tomato
1 small yellow tomato
1 small red tomato
1 green pitted olive
1 black pitted olive

1 Cut one red round tomato into half. Place each half with the cut side down.

2 Cut a section out of the center of the first tomato half by making two symmetrical diagonal cuts. Displace the cut section slightly.

3 Make a parallel cut toward the middle of the tomato slightly apart from the cut section. Make the same cut to the middle of the tomato from the opposite side so that you can again cut out a section. Displace it at the same distance as the first section.

4 Cut out one more section. Displace the last cut section. This is the owl's wing. Repeat steps 2-4 to make the second wing.

6 Cut out a small segment from the center of each half to use as eyebrows. Carve sections as in step 3 but do not displace the segments.

5 Cut the second round tomato in half. These are the eyes.

7 Cut a small segment out of the black olive. This is the pupil.

8 Cut out one more pupil. Insert the pupils into the eyes.

9 Cut a small slice from the small yellow tomato on the diagonal. Cut the same slice from the opposite side.

10 Make a horizontal incision in the remaining piece. Remove the pulp. This is the beak.

11 Place the beak between the eyes. Use the red oval tomato for the body. Lay out the wings on either side.

12 Cut the small oval tomato into quarters. Use two of them as legs. Use the halves of one olive ring as claws.

Rabbit

INGREDIENTS

1 round red tomato

1 small yellow tomato

7 snow peas

1 pitted black olive

1 pitted green olive

2 corn kernels

1 sweet pea

1 Make a horizontal incision in the red tomato.

2 Insert two snow peas into it. These are the ears.

3 Cut the small yellow tomato in half without severing it.

4 Carefully place the yellow tomato cut side down onto the red tomato. These are the eyes.

5 Cut a thin round slice from a black olive. Cut it into two semicircles.

6 These are pupils. Lay the pupils on the eyes.

7 Make a cross incision in a green olive. This is the mouth.

8 Insert two corn kernels into the incision. These are the teeth.

9 Lay the mouth on the head.

10 Put the sweet pea above the mouth. This is the nose. Use the snow peas for the body, legs and arms.

11 Alternatively, you can use additional tomatoes for the body.

Dog

INGREDIENTS

2 round red tomatoes
5 small red tomatoes
1 snow pea
2 pitted black olives

1 pitted green olive
4 corn kernels
2 sweet peas
2 watercress leaves

1 Slice one tomato in half. Slightly displace the top half from the lower one. This is the dog's head.

2 Insert two watercress leaves between the tomato halves. These are the ears.

3 Cut a ring from the black olive for one eye. Cut a ring from the green olive for the second eye. Place the eyes on the head.

4 Insert a sweet pea into the hole of each olive ring for the pupils.

5 Make an incision in the middle of one small tomato. This is the mouth.

6 Insert corn kernels into the incision. These are the teeth.

7 Cut one black olive in half. This is the nose.

8 Place the mouth on the lower part of the head and place the nose on the top.

9 Use the second round tomato for the body. Make legs from the remaining small tomatoes. Use the snow pea for the tail.

23

Boy

INGREDIENTS

- 2 round tomatoes, one larger than the other
- 5 small tomatoes
- 2 pitted black olives
- 1 pitted green olive
- 6 corn kernels
- 1 parsley stalk

1 Make a horizontal incision in the largest tomato. This is the mouth.

2 Cut each corn kernel in half lengthwise, without completely severing the two halves.

3 Insert the kernels so that one half of each hangs from the mouth. These are the teeth.

4 Cut two rings from the green olive. These are the eyes.

5 Cut two round slices from the black olive for pupils. Place the pupils on top of the eyes.

6 Place the eyes on the face. Use a small oblong tomato for the nose.

7 Use two small round tomatoes for the ears. Use the parsley leaves for hair.

8 Use the second round tomato for the body, and two small tomatoes as legs.

9 Make a hole in the corn kernel using a toothpick.

10 Insert a small parsley stalk into the hole. This is an arm.

11 Make another arm and place them against the body.

12 Cut the second black olive in half lengthwise. These are the boots. Place the boots against the legs.

Dragonfly

INGREDIENTS

1 red tomato

3 small yellow tomatoes

1 pitted black olive

2 pitted green olives

1 sweet pea

4 snow peas

1 Cut one green olive lengthwise, without completely severing the two halves.

2 Lay out olive halves cut side down. These are the eyes.

3 Cut a small segment out of the center of each half.

4 Cut the black olive in half lengthwise.

5 From one half of the black olive, cut two segments equal in size to the segments cut out of the green olives.

6 Insert the black olive segments into the green olives. These are the pupils.

7 Place the eyes on the tomato. This is the head.

8 Cut the sweet pea in half.

9 Place it under the eyes. This is the nose.

10 Make the body from the yellow tomatoes.

11 Use snow peas for wings.

Fly

INGREDIENTS
1 red tomato
1 small yellow tomato
1 pitted black olive
4 watercress leaves
parsley stalk

1 Cut the red tomato in half. Slightly displace the top half of the tomato.

2 Cut the yellow tomato in half. These are the eyes. Make an incision in each half for the pupils.

3 Cut the black olive in half. Cut two thin segments from one half. These are the pupils. Insert them into the incisions in the yellow tomato halves. Place the eyes on the lower part of the tomato. Insert a small parsley stalk between them. This is the proboscis. Insert leaves between the halves of the red tomato as wings.

Hedgehog 1

INGREDIENTS

1 oblong tomato

1 pitted black olive

2 pitted green olives

2 small onion rings

2 green chive stalks

arugula leaves

1 Cut the tomato in half lengthwise. Lay one half with cut side down. This is the head.

2 Cut the ends from a black olive. Put them on the head. These are the pupils. Place an onion ring around each pupil for the eyes.

3 Cut the black olive in half lengthwise. Place half against the head. This is the nose. Cut the green olives in half lengthwise. Place them with the cut side down behind the body. These are the legs. Cover them with arugula leaves as shown. These are the hedgehog's needles.

Crocodile

INGREDIENTS

1 round red tomato

5 small red tomatoes

1 pitted black olive

1 pitted green olive

2 corn kernels

1 Cut the top third from the round tomato. Slightly displace the top section. This is the head of the crocodile.

2 Make an incision in half of a small tomato, without completely severing the two quarters. These are the backs of the eyes.

3 Put them on the head.

4 Cut one black and one green olive in half lengthwise. Cut identical segments out of each half.

5 Put a black olive segment in the incision of a green olive half.

6 Cut this half in two. These are the eyes.

7 Put the eyes on the head.

8 Cut a corn kernel in half lengthwise without severing the halves. These are teeth.

9 Lay them on the exposed lower part of the tomato head.

10 Cut the remaining half of a small tomato in two. These are the nostrils.

11 Place three small tomatoes lengthwise against the head. This is the body. Cut one more tomato into quarters. These are the legs.

Duck

INGREDIENTS

2 red tomatoes of
    different size

1 oblong small tomato

1 pitted black olive

1 pitted green olive

1 corn kernel

1 snow pea

parsley stalk

1 Make two incisions on each side of a big round tomato. This is the duck's body.

2 Cut a snow pea in half. Cut the flat edge of each half in a zigzag. These are the wings.

3 Insert the wings into the incisions on the body.

4 Use a smaller round tomato for the head. Make a hole on the side of the same diameter as the oblong small tomato. The latter is the beak.

5 Insert the beak into the hole. This is the head.

6 Make a hole in the bottom of the head with a toothpick and insert a parsley stalk into it for fastening to the body.

7 Put an olive ring on the body for the neck. Insert a toothpick through the olive ring into the tomato.

8 Attach the head to the body.

9 Cut a corn kernel in half, without completely severing. Unfold the halves and attach on the head. These are the eyes.

10 Cut two thin round olive slices for the pupils.

11 Attach them to the eyes.

Hippo

INGREDIENTS

2 red tomatoes of different size
3 oblong small tomatoes
1 pitted black olive
1 pitted green olive

1 corn kernel
1 snow pea
2 watercress leaves

1 Make a vertical incision at the top of a small oblong tomato. This is the head.

2 Insert two leaves into the incision for the ears.

3 Use an apple corer to make a hole in the larger round tomato the same diameter as the oblong tomato.

4 Insert the oblong tomato into the hole. This is the head and muzzle.

5 Slice a corn kernel in half, without completely severing the two halves. These are the eyes.

6 Cut a thin round slice from an olive. Cut it in half. These are the pupils.

7 Unfold the halves of the corn kernel eyes and place pupils on eyes.

8 Place the eyes on the head.

9 Cut two rings from a green olive. Place them on the muzzle. These are the nostrils.

10 Use a larger round tomato for the body.

11 Crosscut the other small tomatoes in half for the legs.

12 Place them against the body.

Deer

INGREDIENTS

2 round red tomatoes of
    different size

2 oblong small tomatoes

2 pitted black olives

1 pitted green olive

2 arugula leaves

parsley stalk

1 In a round tomato, make a hole of the same diameter as an oblong small tomato. This is the muzzle.

2 Make a vertical incision in the top of a small tomato. This is the head.

3 Insert the other end of the head into the hole in the muzzle.

4 Cut a thin slice from an oblong tomato.

5 Cut the slice in half lengthwise. These are the ears.

6 Insert the ears into the incision on the head.

7 Insert arugula leaves into the same incision. These are the antlers.

8 Slice a green olive in half, leaving a thin section uncut.

9 Place the halves with the cut side down. These are the eyes. Cut thin segments out of the eyes. Cut the same-sized sections out of a black olive. These are the pupils.

11 Cut a black olive in half lengthwise. Cut each half in two. These are the hooves. Make a slit in each hoof.

10 Insert the pupils into the eyes. Place the eyes on the head.

12 Insert a small parsley stalk into each hoof. These are the legs.

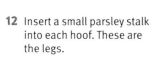

13 Use a large round tomato as a body. Place the legs against the body.

Swan

INGREDIENTS

4 round tomatoes of different sizes

1 pitted black olive

1 pitted green olive

1 sweet pea

1 corn kernel

watercress leaves

parsley stalk

1 Make a hole in a round tomato with a wooden skewer. This is the head. Insert a small piece of parsley stalk into the hole for fastening on a beak.

2 Skewer a corn kernel onto the stalk. This is the beak.

3 Make an incision in a sweet pea, leaving a thin section uncut. Unfold the sweet pea halves. These are the eyes.

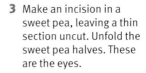

4 Cut tiny dots from the black olive. These are pupils.

5 Place the pupils on the eyes. Place the eyes on the head.

6 Cut two side slices from a larger whole tomato. Cut a slice from the middle of the tomato into two parts. These are the wings.

7 Put one of the side slices with the cut side up and lay watercress leaves on it for a tail.

8 Cover with the second slice, cut side down. This is the body. Place the wings against the body.

10 Insert a small piece of parsley stalk for fastening.

11 Cut two rings from the green olive.

9 Use a smaller round tomato for the lower part of the neck. Make a hole in the top.

12 Using the parsley stalk or a toothpick stack the neck pieces and head with an olive rings between them.

Ladybug

INGREDIENTS

1 round tomato
2 pitted black olives
1 green olive
1 slice white onion
1 corn kernel
2 green chive stalks

1 Cut the tomato into three slices.

2 Cut the middle slice in half. These are the wings.

3 Lay one side slice cut side up. This is the head.

4 Place one whole black olive as the nose. Cut three green olive rings. Place one on the head as the mouth.

5 Make an incision in both peas. Cut sections out of black olive of a size to fit in the incision. Insert the pupils in the peas.

6 Insert the pupils in the green olive rings.

7 Place the eyes on the head.

8 Insert two small parsley stalks between the eyes. These are the antennae.

9 Put the other half of the tomato cut side down. This is the body. Place the wings on the body. Cut six tiny round dots from a black olive.

10 Arrange the black olive dots on the wings.

11 Cut the corn kernels in half. Use the halves and chive stalks for feet and legs.

Cat 1

INGREDIENTS
1 round tomato
1 small tomato
1 sweet pea
2 pitted green olives
1 pitted black olive
1 snow pea
2 green chive stalks

1 Cut the round tomato into three slices.

2 Cut the middle slice in half. These are the ears.

3 Put one of the side slices with the cut side down. This is the body. Put the second slice against it with the cut side up. This is the head.

4 Place the ears on the head.

5 Cut a ring from a green olive. Lay it on the head. This is the mouth.

6 Cut a small tomato in half lengthwise. Place the halves on the head. These are the cheeks.

7 Cut thin segments out of the black olive for the pupils.

8 Cut a green olive in half lengthwise. These are the eyes.

9 Cut segments of the same size as the pupils out of the eyes.

10 Place the pupils in the cut hollows of the eyes. Place the eyes on the head.

11 Add the snow pea as a tail and the chive stalks as legs. Place the sweet pea between the eyes and cheeks as a nose.

Bulldog

INGREDIENTS

1 tomato
2 small tomatoes
2 black olives
1 pitted green olive
1 snow pea
2 corn kernels
1 onion ring

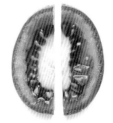

1 Cut the round tomato into three slices.

2 Cut the middle slice in half. These are the cheeks.

3 An onion ring is required as a base.

4 Place a side slice of the tomato on the base, cut side up. This is the head.

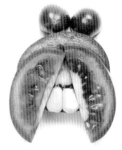

5 Place the cheeks on the head. Between the cheeks, insert the two corn kernels. These are the teeth.

6 Cut a small tomato in half horizontally.

7 Put these against the head. These are the eyes.

8 Cut two rings from a green olive. Cut two round dots from a black olive. Place these on the olive rings. These are the pupils.

9 Place the pupils on the eyes. Place a whole black olive on top for the nose.

10 Cut a small tomato in half lengthwise. Cut one half in two. These are the ears. Place the ears against the head.

11 Cut a snow pea in half, then cut a leg out of each half, as shown.

12 Place the second side slice from the round tomato next to the head. This is the body. Place the legs against the body. Use half of a small tomato for the tail.

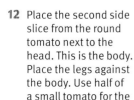

Sheep

INGREDIENTS

1 whole tomato

2 small tomatoes

1 small yellow
tomato

1 pitted black olive

1 pitted green olive

4 corn kernels

1 onion ring

watercress leaves

4 chive stalks

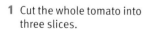

1 Cut the whole tomato into three slices.

2 Cut the middle slice in half. These are the ears.

3 An onion ring is required as a base.

4 Place a side slice of the tomato on the base, cut side up. Place the corn kernels along one edge. These are the teeth.

5 Place the second side slice of the tomato on top, cut side down. This is the muzzle.

6 Cut two circles from a green olive. Place them on the muzzle. These are the nostrils.

7 Cut a small tomato in half lengthwise. Place the halves, cut side up, next to the muzzle. These are the base for the eyes.

8 Place the ears against the eye bases.

9 Cut a yellow tomato in half. These are the eyes. Make a cut in each half for the pupils.

10 Cut thin segments out of a black olive for the pupils.

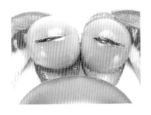

11 Insert the pupils into the eyes. Put each eye on the base.

12 Make the body from watercress and use chive stalks for legs. Make hooves with black olive rings cut in quarters.

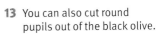

13 You can also cut round pupils out of the black olive.

Rooster

INGREDIENTS

1 whole tomato
2 small red tomatoes
1 small yellow tomato
1 pitted green olive
1 pitted black olive
1 onion ring
chive stalks
1 snow pea

1 Cut the whole tomato into three slices.

2 Cut the middle slice in half. These are the wings.

3 An onion ring is required as a base. Place a side slice of the tomato on the base. This is the head.

4 Cut the yellow tomato in half crosswise. These are the eyes.

5 Cut two round slices from the black olive. These are the pupils.

6 Place the pupils on the eyes. Place the eyes on the head.

7 Cut a beak out of the snow pea. Place the beak on the head.

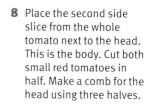

8 Place the second side slice from the whole tomato next to the head. This is the body. Cut both small red tomatoes in half. Make a comb for the head using three halves.

9 Cut the chive stalks into six short slices for the feet and two long slices for the legs.

10 Put the legs against the body and arrange the feet.

11 Make a tail from three chive stalks.

12 Attach the wings.

Lion

INGREDIENTS

1 whole tomato

2 small red
    tomatoes

1 small yellow
    tomato

1 pitted black olive

lettuce leaves

1 chive stalk

8 corn kernels

1 Lay out lettuce leaves in the form of a mane.

2 Cut the whole tomato in half lengthwise. Lay one half on the mane cut side up. This is the head.

3 Cut a small red tomato in half. Cut one half in two. These are the ears.

4 Place the ears against the head.

5 Cut the yellow tomato in half. Place them on the head cut side down. These are the eyes.

6 Cut two round slices from the olive for the pupils.

7 Place the pupils on the eyes. Place two corn kernels on the edge of the head. These are the teeth.

8 Put half of a small tomato on top of the bottom half of the head, covering the corn kernels. This is the muzzle.

9 Cut off a half of the black olive for the nose.

10 Place the nose on the muzzle. Put the other half of the whole tomato next to the mane. This is the body.

12 Cut a small red tomato in half lengthwise. These are the legs. Add corn kernels as toes.

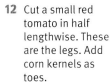

11 Use a chive stalk for the tail. Place a small slice of lettuce leaf at the tip for the tuft.

13 You could also use snow peas for the body, legs and feet.

Parrot

INGREDIENTS

1 whole tomato
1 sweet pea
1 pitted black olive
1 pitted green olive
3 snow peas

1 Cut the whole tomato into three slices.

2 Cut the middle slice in half. Arrange these in the form of an open beak.

3 Put a side slice on top cut side down. This is the head.

4 Cut a ring from the green olive. Place the sweet pea in the olive ring. This is the eye.

5 Cut a tiny circle from the black olive. This is the pupil.

6 Place the pupil on the eye. Place the eye on the head.

7 The second side slice of the tomato is the body. Make a small incision on the side for fastening a wing.

8 Place the body next to the head. Insert two snow peas under it for the tail and one wing.

9 Insert the third snow pea into the incision to make the second wing.

10 Cut legs out of the black olive.

11 Place the legs against the body.

12 Cut an olive ring in quarters for the toes. Place one quarter against each leg.

Fox

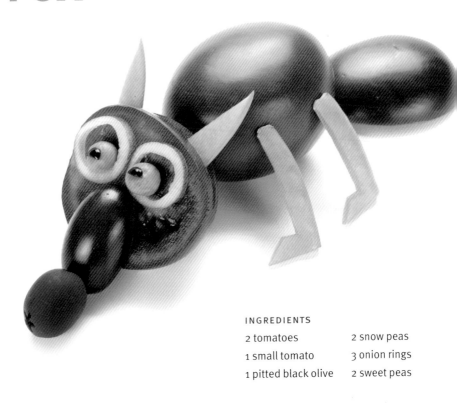

INGREDIENTS

2 tomatoes	2 snow peas
1 small tomato	3 onion rings
1 pitted black olive	2 sweet peas

1 Cut a tomato in half lengthwise.

2 One half is the head. Make an incision in it for the ears.

3 The second half is the tail. Place the second whole tomato against it. This is the body.

4 Next to the body, place an onion ring as a base for the head.

5 Rest the head, cut side up, on the onion ring and against the body.

6 Cut the snow peas into two parts. Cut out legs as indicated.

7 The two cut triangles are the ears. Insert the ears into the head incision.

8 Rest a small tomato against the head for the muzzle. Place two onion rings on the head.

9 Slice a small round from the olive. Cut the round in half. These are the pupils.

 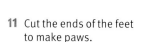 

10 Cut a sweet pea in half. Place inside the onion rings on the head. These are the eyes. Place pupils on top.

11 Cut the ends of the feet to make paws.

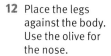

12 Place the legs against the body. Use the olive for the nose.

Skeleton

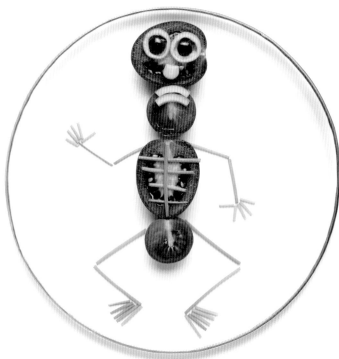

INGREDIENTS

1 small round tomato
1 oblong tomato
1 black olive
5 small onion rings
1 corn kernel
chive stalks

1 Cut a tomato in half lengthwise.

2 Place half of the tomato on an onion ring base. This is the skull.

3 Slice two small rounds from the olive.

4 Place the rounds on the skull. Place two small onion rings on top. These are the eye sockets.

56

5 Use a corn kernel for the nose. Place one more onion ring next to the skull.

6 Cut the small tomato in half. Place one half on the onion ring, cut side up. It is the jaw.

7 Cut half of an onion ring in two. Place these slices in parallel on the jaw. This is the mouth.

8 Place one more onion ring as a support next to the jaw.

9 Lay the second half of the oblong tomato on it to make the cut side up. Make ribs from chive slices. Place one more onion ring next to the body.

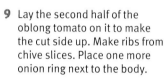

10 Put half of the small tomato on the onion ring. This is the pelvis.

11 Make arms, fingers and legs from chive slices.

You can give the skeleton any desired position.

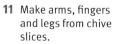

Bee

INGREDIENTS

2 red tomatoes of different sizes
3 yellow tomatoes
1 black olive

3 onion rings
1 chive stalk

1 Cut two yellow tomatoes in half lengthwise.

2 Place one half with the cut side down.

58

3 Rest an onion ring against the yellow tomato.

4 Place another yellow tomato half against the onion ring.

5 Rest another onion ring against this half.

6 Lay a third yellow tomato half on the onion ring, then rest the third onion ring against the tomato. Place the final half of the yellow tomato against the onion ring. This is the body.

7 The third yellow tomato is the head. Using a toothpick, make a hole in the head for the proboscis.

8 Insert a piece of chive stalk as the proboscis. Place the head against the body.

9 Slice two rounds from the olive. These are the eyes.

10 Place the eyes on the head.

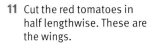

11 Cut the red tomatoes in half lengthwise. These are the wings.

12 Place the wings against the body.

Goblin

INGREDIENTS

1 red tomato

2 small yellow tomatoes

2 small red tomatoes

1 pitted black olive

1 pitted green olive

3 onion rings

1 snow pea

14 corn kernels

1 Cut the red tomato in half.

2 Place one half of the tomato cut side down. This is the body.

3 Cut the yellow tomatoes in half. Place them against the body. These are the arms and legs.

4 Use 12 corn kernels for fingers and toes.

5 Place an onion ring on top of the body. This is the neck.

6 The second half of the red tomato is the head. Make an incision in it and place cut side up on the neck. This is the mouth.

7 Insert two corn kernels into the incision. These are the teeth.

8 Place the head on the neck.

9 Place a snow pea on top of the head. Place two onion rings over top of this.

10 Place the two small red tomatoes on top of the onion rings. These are the eyes.

11 Slice two rounds from the black olive.

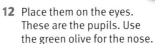

12 Place them on the eyes. These are the pupils. Use the green olive for the nose.

Owl

INGREDIENTS

1 red tomato

1 small yellow tomato

1 small red tomato

1 black olive

1 pitted green olive

3 onion rings

1 dill stalk

1 Cut the red tomato in half.

2 One half of the tomato is the head. Make a engthwise incision on one side.

3 Place the head, cut side up, on an onion ring. Insert dill stalks into the incision. These are the ears.

4 Place two onion rings on the head.

5 Cut the yellow tomato in half. These are the eyes. Place them in the onion rings, cut side up.

6 Slice two small rounds from the black olive. Place them on the eyes. These are the pupils.

7 Cut the small red tomato in half lengthwise.

8 Cut one half in two. These are the legs. Cut two small sections from the second half. These are the wings. The remaining triangular slice is the beak.

9 Place the beak on the head.

10 Place the other half of the red tomato next to the head, cut side down. This is the body.

11 Place legs and wings against the body.

12 Cut a green olive ring in half. These are the toes.

Tiger

INGREDIENTS
1 red tomato
1 small yellow tomato
3 small red tomatoes
2 pitted black olives
2 onion rings
3 corn kernels
6 chive stalks

1 Cut the red tomato in half.

2 Place an onion ring as a base. Place half of the tomato on it, cut side up. Place another onion ring next to the tomato.

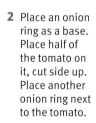

3 Lay the second tomato half on the onion ring. This is the tiger's head. Use two small red tomatoes for the ears.

4 Slice two small rounds from an olive. Put them on the head. Place two onion rings on top. These are the eyes.

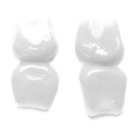

5 Cut the third small red tomato in half. Place it on the muzzle. This is the nose.

6 Make an incision in two corn kernels, leaving a thin section uncut. Unfold the halves of the kernel. These are the teeth.

7 Place the teeth along the bottom of the muzzle. Surround with an onion ring. This is the mouth.

8 Insert chive stalks under the nose for whiskers.

9 Place a full onion slice next to the head and muzzle. This is the body.

10 Make legs and a tail from onion ring strands.

11 Cut the yellow tomato in half. Cut one half in two. These are the paws. Place against the legs.

12 Attach a corn kernel to the tail for the tuft.

Zebra

INGREDIENTS

2 red tomatoes of
   different sizes
4 small red tomatoes
2 pitted black olives
1 pitted green olive
1 red onion
4 corn kernels

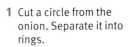

1 Cut a circle from the onion. Separate it into rings.

2 Cut a tomato in half.

3 Choose a small onion ring. Place half of the tomato on it. This is the zebra's muzzle.

4 Cut a small tomato in half lengthwise.

5 Cut one half in two. This is the mouth. Place it on the muzzle.

6 Insert corn kernels into the mouth. These are the teeth. Cut two rings from a green olive, and place above the mouth. These are the nostrils.

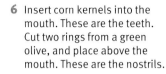

7 Place another onion ring next to the muzzle. Place the second tomato half on the onion ring. This is the head.

8 Slice two small rounds from the black olive. Place them on the head. These are the eyes.

9 Use two small tomatoes for the ears. Another small tomato will be the neck. Use a slightly larger whole tomato as the body.

10 Cut the onion rings in half and lay the strips over the body.

11 Make a tail and legs in the same way.

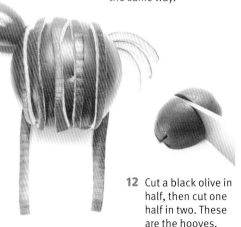

12 Cut a black olive in half, then cut one half in two. These are the hooves.

13 Put them against the legs.

Pig

INGREDIENTS

1 red tomato

1 small yellow tomato

2 small red tomatoes
of different sizes

2 pitted black olives

1 pitted green olive

3 onion rings

1 snow pea

1 sweet pea

1 chive stalk

1 Cut a tomato in half.

2 In one half, make an incision on the side. Place this half on an onion ring, cut side up. This is the head.

3 Cut two triangular slices from the snow pea. These are the ears. Insert them into the incision.

4 Place two small onion rings on the head. Cut the sweet pea in half, and insert the halves into the onion rings. These are the eyes.

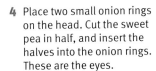

5 Slice two tiny rounds from a black olive. Place them on the sweet peas. These are the pupils.

6 Cut the yellow tomato in half. Place one half on the head under the eyes, cut side up. This is the snout.

7 Cut two rings from the green olive.

8 Place these on the snout. Cut two small slices of chive. These are the mouth.

9 Place the second half of the tomato next to the head, cut side down. This is the body.

10 Cut the small red tomatoes in half lengthwise.

11 Place them against the body. These are the arms and legs.

12 Cut a black olive in half. Cut each half into two parts. These are the hooves.

13 Place them against the arms and legs.

Zombie

INGREDIENTS

1 round tomato
1 oblong tomato
1 small yellow tomato
1 small red tomato
1 black olive
5 onion rings
3 snow peas
arugula leaves

1 Lay out the arugula in the form of a hairstyle. Place two onion rings underneath.

2 Cut the oblong tomato in half. Place each half on an onion ring, cut side up. These are the bases for the eyes.

3 Place the round tomato next to the eyes. This is the bottom part of the face. Use two more onion rings for the ears.

4 Cut the yellow tomato in half.

5 Place each half on an eye base, cut side up. These are the eyes.

6 Slice two small rounds from the black olive. Place them on the eyes. These are the pupils.

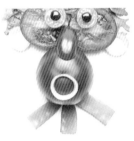

7 Use a small onion ring for the mouth and half of a small red tomato for the nose.

8 Cut two snow peas in half. Cut one half lengthwise. These are the legs.

9 Make a body and arms from the remaining halves.

10 Cut two tips from the third snow pea. Cut hands out of each tip.

11 Place the hands against the arms and the legs against the body.

12 You can also make other poses.

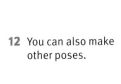

Wolf

INGREDIENTS

1 round tomato

1 oblong tomato

2 tomatoes of different sizes

2 pitted black olives

3 onion rings

1 snow pea

12 sweet peas

4 chive stalks

1 The round tomato is the body. Cut a small slice off the bottom of the tomato to make a flat base. Use an onion ring on top for the neck.

2 Cut the oblong tomato in half. Place one half on the neck, cut side up. This is the head.

3 Cut the smaller of the two other tomatoes in half.

4 Cut one half in two.

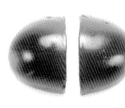

5 Place them on the head with the cut side down. These are the ears.

6 Cut the second small tomato in half. Use to make a muzzle and eye base.

7 Place two onion rings over the eye base. These are the eyes.

8 Cut two small rounds from a black olive.

9 Place them in the onion rings. These are the pupils.

10 Cut the other olive in half. Place one half over the muzzle. This is the nose.

11 Cut chive stalks into four identical pieces for the legs. Place the legs against the body.

12 Arrange three sweet peas at the end of each leg for the paws. Use the snow pea for the tail.

Hedgehog 2

INGREDIENTS

1 oblong tomato
1 small red tomato
2 small yellow tomatoes
1 pitted black olive
1 pitted green olive
3 onion rings
lettuce leaves

1 Lay out lettuce leaves as shown in the photo. These are the quills of the hedgehog. Place an onion ring as a base.

2 Cut the oblong tomato in half.

3 Lay one half on the onion ring, cut side up. This is the head. Use the second half of the tomato for the body, cut side down.

4 Slice two small rounds from the black olive.

5 Place them on the head. These are the pupils.

6 Place an onion ring around each pupil. These are the eyes.

7 Cut a ring from the green olive. This is the mouth.

8 Cut the small red tomato in half. Lay one half on the head, cut side down. This is the muzzle.

9 Slice another round from the olive. This is the nose.

10 Place the nose on the muzzle.

11 Cut yellow tomatoes in half.

12 Rest them against the body with the cut side down. These are the legs.

Pirate

INGREDIENTS

1 round tomato
1 oblong tomato
1 small yellow tomato
2 pitted black olives
2 pitted green olives
3 onion rings
5 corn kernels
1 snow pea
lettuce leaves
chive stalks

1 Cut the round tomato in half. On one half, make an incision on the side. This is the head.

2 Use an onion ring as a base. Place the head on the base. Insert a lettuce leaf into the incision. This is the pirate's hair.

3 Cut a green olive in half lengthwise. These are the ears. Place them against the head on either side.

4 Cut a narrow segment out of a black olive. Cut the other green olive in half. In one half, cut out a section of the same size as the segment from the black olive.

5 Insert the black olive segment into the green olive. This is an eye. Place the eye on the head. Cut a black olive in half, then one half in two. Place next to the eye. This is the eye patch.

6 Put the yellow tomato under the eyes. This is the nose. Place an onion ring as a base below the face. Place the second half of the round tomato on top.

7 Cover the tomato with a lettuce leaf. This is the beard. Place a small onion ring on top. This is the mouth.

8 Use the oblong tomato as the body. Place three corn kernels on it as buttons.

9 Put two chive slices against the body. These are the arms. Use two corn kernels for hands.

10 Cut a small slice from the snow pea. Insert a small piece of chive stalk into it. Place against the body. This is the wooden leg.

11 The remaining slice of the snow pea is the other leg.

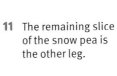

12 Cut a black olive in half. Cut one half lengthwise and cut a small slice from the second half. Make a high boot from the two parts.

13 Place the high boot against the leg. Put a square slice cut from the onion ring against the wooden leg.

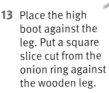

Skier

INGREDIENTS

2 round tomatoes of
  different sizes
5 small red tomatoes
3 small yellow tomatoes
2 pitted black olives
1 pitted green olive
4 sweet peas
onion rings
parsley leaves
10 corn kernels
2 snow peas

1 The largest tomato is the head.

2 Use one of the small red tomatoes as a nose and place on the head.

3 Cut a green olive in half.

4 Place the olive halves on the head, cut side up. These are the eyes.

5 Slice two rounds from a black olive. These are the pupils.

6 Place the pupils on the eyes. Choose a small onion ring for the mouth.

7 Use parsley leaves for the moustache. Make a cone cap from the onion rings. The middle of the onion circle is a pompon.

8 Use two yellow tomatoes for the ears. Use the other round tomato for the body. Place a line of sweet peas along the body as buttons.

9 Put two oval tomatoes against the body as arms. Cut a yellow tomato in half. These are the hands.

10 Use the corn kernels as fingers.

11 Put two more oval tomatoes against the body as legs.

12 Cut both snow peas lengthwise into two strips. Choose two skis from them.

13 Cut an olive in half. These are the boots.

14 Place the skis against the legs and lay the boots on top.

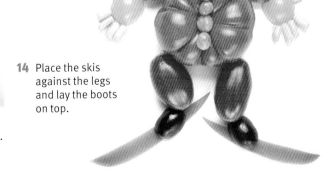

Clown

INGREDIENTS

2 round tomatoes of
different sizes

1 small round tomato

2 small oblong tomatoes

1 small yellow tomato

2 pitted black olives

1 small red onion

10 corn kernels

parsley leaves

lettuce leaves

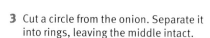

3 Cut a circle from the onion. Separate it
into rings, leaving the middle intact.

1 The largest
tomato is the
head.

2 Use the small
round tomato for
the nose.

4 Cut one of the
rings in two.
These are the
eyebrows.

5 Slice two tiny rounds from a black olive. These are the eyes.

6 Cut slices from two onion rings. Place two together as lips.

7 Place a parsley leaf underneath as a beard.

8 Cut a green olive in half lengthwise. These are the ears.

9 Place the ears against the head. Arrange a hairstyle using the lettuce leaves.

10 Make a hat using a circle and thicker slice of onion.

11 Use the second round tomato for the body. Make arms from the cut onion ring.

12 Cut a yellow tomato in half. These are the hands.

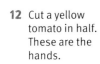

13 Use corn kernels as fingers.

14 Put two more red tomatoes against the body as legs. Make boots from olive halves.

Goat

INGREDIENTS

2 tomatoes
1 small red tomato
1 small yellow tomato
1 pitted black olive
2 pitted green olives
1 onion ring
1 snow pea
2 chive stalks

1 Cut a tomato in half.

2 The bottom half is the head.

4 Cut two tips from the snow pea at an angle. These are the ears.

3 Place the other half of the tomato on top. This is the muzzle. Cut the onion ring into small pieces and use two for the horns. Cut the yellow tomato in half and use these as eyes.

5 Place them under the yellow tomato halves.

6 Slice two tiny rounds from the black olive. These are the pupils.

7 Place the pupils on the eyes. Use two rings of a green olive for the nostrils.

8 Use two small pieces of onion ring under the nose for a mouth.

9 Use the remaining middle part of the snow pea as a beard. Use the other tomato as the body.

10 Use chive stalks as legs.

11 Cut a green olive in half. These are the hooves.

12 Put hoofs next to legs and use a small tomato for the tail.

Mouse

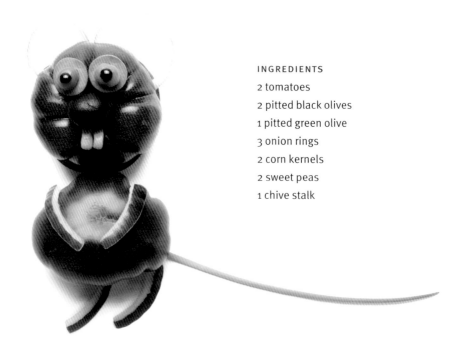

INGREDIENTS

2 tomatoes

2 pitted black olives

1 pitted green olive

3 onion rings

2 corn kernels

2 sweet peas

1 chive stalk

1 Cut one tomato in half.

2 On the bottom half place two onion rings. These are the ears.

3 Cover with the top half of the tomato. This is the muzzle.

4 Place two corn kernels on the muzzle as teeth.

5 Use a black olive for the nose.

6 Cut two rings from the green olive.

7 Place a sweet pea in the middle of each olive ring. These are the eyes.

8 Slice two tiny rounds from a black olive. These are the pupils. Place the pupils on the eyes.

9 Place the eyes on the muzzle. Place the other tomato next to the head. This is the body.

10 Cut a big onion ring into four parts. These are the arms and legs.

11 Lay out the arms and legs along the body.

12 Use a chive stalk for the tail.

Cat 2

INGREDIENTS

2 large tomatoes
1 small red tomato
2 small yellow tomatoes
1 pitted black olive
3 pitted green olives
8 corn kernels
3 chive stalks

1 The largest tomato is the head.

2 Place the small red tomato on the head. This is the nose.

3 Cut out a narrow segment from each green olive.

4 Cut the same-sized segments from a black olive.

5 Insert black olive segments into the cuts on the green olives. These are the eyes. Place the eyes on the head.

6 Put three chive stalks under the nose. These are the whiskers.

7 Cut a ring from a green olive to use as the mouth.

8 Cut a thick segment from the second tomato.

9 Cut the segment into two parts. These are the ears.

10 Place the ears against the head.

11 Cut one more segment for a tail.

12 The cut tomato is the body. Place the tail against the body.

13 Use yellow tomatoes for legs and corn kernels for paws.

Crayfish

INGREDIENTS

6 small oblong red tomatoes
1 pitted black olive
2 chive stalks

1 Slice two tiny rounds from a black olive. These are the eyes.

2 Place the eyes on a small tomato. This is the head.

3 Use a slightly bigger tomato for the body.

4 Make crosscuts in the third tomato, not cutting all the way through.

5 Place against the body. This is the tail.

6 Cut three side slices from the fourth tomato. Place them under the tail.

7 Cut the fifth tomato into rounds. Choose three rounds and cut each circle into half.

8 Remove seeds and pulp from the middle of each circle. These are the side legs.

9 Cut the sixth tomato in half lengthwise. Cut a thin slice from one half.

10 Make a cut off the edge of this slice. Remove pulp and seeds. This is a foreleg.

11 Repeat step 10 with the second half of the tomato.

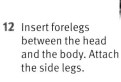

12 Insert forelegs between the head and the body. Attach the side legs.

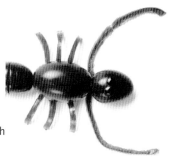

13 Cut claws out of side slices.

14 Place the claws against the forelegs. Place chive stalks under the head as antennae.

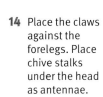

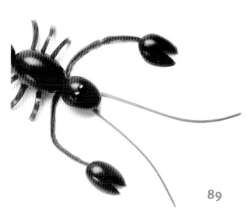

Crab

INGREDIENTS

1 round tomato

5 small oblong red
tomatoes

1 black olive

1 pitted green olive

1 Cut an oval tomato in
half lengthwise.

2 Cut each half into two,
leaving a thin section
uncut from the one end.

3 Unfold the quarters.
These are legs.

4 Put the legs against the round tomato. This is the crab's body.

5 Make three more pairs of legs from three oblong tomatoes.

6 Cut one more whole tomato into halves and make cuts in them. These are claws.

7 Place the claws against the forelegs.

8 Cut tips off of both ends of the green olive. Cut the middle part of the olive into two rings, leaving a thin section uncut.

9 Unfold the rings.

10 Place them on the crab. These are the eyes.

11 Slice two rounds from the black olive. These are the pupils.

12 Place the pupils on the eyes.

Centipede

INGREDIENTS

1 large tomato

4 small round tomatoes

1 small oblong tomato

2 small yellow tomatoes

1 pitted black olive

corn kernels

1 onion slice

1 Cut a quarter section out of the large tomato. This is the head.

2 Cut similar sections out of the yellow tomatoes. These are the eyes.

3 Cut the olive in half.

4 Cut one half into two. These are the pupils.

5 Insert the pupils into the eyes.

6 Place the eyes on the cut in the large tomato.

7 Separate an onion circle into rings; lay them out in a line behind the head as supports.

8 Put small tomatoes on them to make a centipede's body.

9 Cut big onion rings into slices. These are the legs.

10 Arrange the legs on both sides of the centipede's body.

11 Place a corn kernel against each leg as a high boot.

Teapot

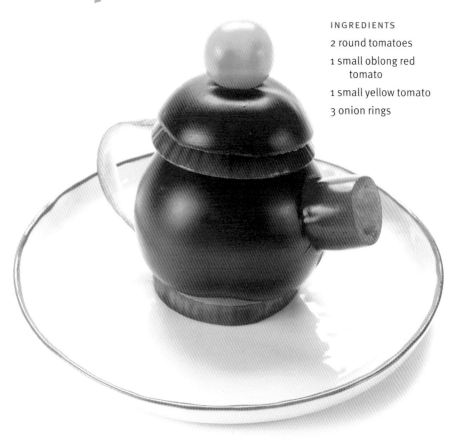

INGREDIENTS

2 round tomatoes

1 small oblong red tomato

1 small yellow tomato

3 onion rings

1 Using an apple corer, cut a hole in the tomato.

2 Choose a small tomato of the same diameter as this hole. Cut the top off the tomato.

3 Remove seeds and pulp from the middle of the small tomato. This is the spout.

4 Insert the spout into the hole in the round tomato. This is the body of the teapot.

5 Use an onion ring as a base. Place the teapot on the base.

6 Make a cut in the second ring of onion. This is the handle.

7 Insert one end of the handle between the bottom of the teapot and the base.

8 Fix another end of the handle with the third onion ring.

9 Cut a broad slice from the base of the other round tomato.

10 Remove pulp from the middle. This is the lid of the teapot.

11 Put the lid on the teapot.

12 Put a yellow tomato on top of the lid.

A FIREFLY BOOK

Published by Firefly Books Ltd. 2016

Copyright © 2016 Good Mood Editions Gmbh
Text copyright © 2016 Iryna Stepanova, Sergiy Kabachenko
Images copyright© 2016 Iryna Stepanova, Sergiy Kabachenko

All rights reserved. No part of this publication may be reproduced, stored in a retrieval system, or transmitted in any form or by any means, electronic, mechanical, photocopying, recording or otherwise, without the prior written permission of the Publisher.

First printing

PUBLISHER CATALOGING-IN-PUBLICATION DATA (U.S.)
Names: Stepanova, Iryna, author. | Kabachenko, Sergiy, author.
Title: Tomato creatures : make your own / Iryna Stepanova, Sergiy Kabachenko.
Description: Richmond Hill, Ontario, Canada : Firefly Books, 2016. | Series: Make Your Own | Summary: Food presentation skills for cooks, chefs, and parents are provided with step by step instructions and photographs of each step.
Identifiers: ISBN 978-1- 77085-856- 5 (hardcover)
Subjects: LCSH: Cooking (Tomatoes). | Food presentation. | Garnishes (Cooking).
Classification: LCC TX740.5S747 |DDC 641.819 – dc23

LIBRARY AND ARCHIVES CANADA CATALOGUING IN PUBLICATION
Stepanova, Iryna, author
Tomato creatures : make your own / Iryna Stepanova and Sergiy Kabachenko.
(Make your own ; 4)
ISBN 978-1-77085-856-5 (hardback)
1. Food craft. 2. Food presentation. 3. Cooking (Garnishes).
4. Cooking (Tomatoes). I. Kabachenko, Sergiy, author II. Title.
TX740.5.S78 2016   745.5   C2016-903719-3

Published in the United States by
Firefly Books (U.S.) Inc.
P.O. Box 1338, Ellicott Station
Buffalo, New York 14205

Published in Canada by
Firefly Books Ltd.
50 Staples Avenue, Unit 1
Richmond Hill, Ontario L4B 0A7

Cover and interior design: Peter Ross / Counterpunch Inc.

Printed in China

The publisher gratefully acknowledges the financial support for our publishing program by the Government of Canada through the Canada Book Fund as administered by the Department of Canadian Heritage.

FASKEN LEARNING RESOURCE CENTER

9000087361

TX
740.5
.S74
2016

Stepanova, Iryna, author,
photographer.
Tomato creatures : make your
own /